Tawanna Heyward-Bey & LaTania Michelle

Get Certified

Learn The Basics and Benefits
of Becoming A *"Certified"*
Business Owner

Tawanna Heyward-Bey & LaTania Michelle

Get Certified

Learn The Basics and Benefits of Becoming A "*Certified*" Business Owner

Possibility
Publishing

Praise for Tawanna Heyward-Bey

"Before meeting and building a relationship with Tawanna, I had no knowledge or idea that minority business certification existed. Through her mentorship, I gained valuable knowledge about certification that has increased my business revenues.

Before Tawanna shared the value of certification with me, I was working hard with little results. I had a few small contracts but the certification has opened the door to a new world of opportunities for larger contracts.

With her business resources and coaching through the process, I was able to partner with a major company on a large contract with a school district; which has made a powerful impact in my business. I am thrilled and thankful to say that we are two years in, with a signed contract for another three years to go."

Jennifer Rivers-Randall, CEO/Owner
Absolute Resource Solutions

"Tawanna Heyward-Bey is the definition of a true entrepreneur. As a business owner she has reached new heights and positioned herself as a leader in her industry. She has also continued to be a strong advocate for the D/M/WBE industry by providing avenues for business owners to educate themselves on how to leverage their business and make their talents profitable.

I have had the pleasure of working with Tawanna through the Greater Southwest Black Chamber of Commerce, where she is a Board Director. As a Director she has continued to promote economic development and the inclusion of programs which utilize D/M/WBE firms. Her efforts are innumerable and motives genuine."

Sheena Morgan
Small Business Program Coordinator

"I met Tawanna years ago while sourcing Business Development professionals within a North Texas IT placement firm. She was (and continues to be) extremely professional, engaging, motivated, honest, a good listener and conscientiously meticulous.
It was evident right away she was going to be successful so I decided to retain her contact information.

Since then, things have come full circle. I've had the opportunity to work with and work for Tawanna on very large projects and extremely competitive business proposals. Her public speaking, networking and partnership-building skills seem to be what immediately sets her apart from the crowd. She prepares, thinks through and means exactly what she says and then delivers on it"

Ronald Redden
Fulcrum Consulting

I've had the pleasure of having Tawanna Heyward-Bey as a mentor/business coach. My search on Women-Owned Small Business (WOSB) certifications led me to find a YouTube video posted by LaTania Michelle and Tawanna Heyward-Bey on the subject.

I immediately reached out. The first encounter was electrifying! These women are extremely knowledgeable about business, networking, marketing and the MBE/WBE process. They were and still are huge supporters of my personal / business goals, positive mentors, and well versed motivational business coaches.

Tawanna is passionate about empowering others as well as keeping them steadfast on moving forward. Both of these ladies are true gems and inspirational, truly an honor to have worked with them and having them in my corner!

DaVonda St.Clair MBA, MSc ITM, PRINCE2
Top Secret Cleared IT Professional

Praise for LaTania Michelle

If you are looking to open your world to new opportunities, moving to the next level of success or expanding your sources of income, LaTania Michelle is your guide. With a unique grasp of the message your customers, strategic partners and sponsors need to hear to say "Yes", LaTania's wisdom can only guide your business in one direction, Up! Take advantage of her knowledge while you still can.

Maureen O'Crean, MBA
Business consultant, author, publisher and Harvard Graduate

Before my coaching session with LaTania Michelle, not only had I completely lost sight of who I was and the vision that God had for my life or how to publish my book. LaTania Michelle shined so much light on the entire process and made it seem much easier; she is a wealth of information and really knows what she is talking about.

LaTania Michelle's expertise and passion as well as the obvious care she has for those she is coaching, will help you break through to the place where you are confident that you can do anything!"

Pamela Palmer, Author of "God's Word is God's Medicine to You"

Warning – Disclaimer

The purpose of this book is to educate and entertain. The author and/or publisher do not guarantee that anyone following these techniques, suggestions, tips, ideas, or strategies will become successful.

The author and/or publisher shall have neither liability nor responsibility to anyone with respect to any loss or damage caused, or alleged to be caused, directly or indirectly by the information contained in this book.

Possibility Publishing
3940 Marine Ave. Suite #A
Lawndale, Ca 90260
www.possibilitypublishing.org

Limits of Liability and Disclaimer of Warranty

DEDICATIONS

To my dear sons Michael, Barry, William and CJ who inspire me everyday to pull up my bootstraps and keep living the dream of true entrepreneurship.

A special thanks to LaTania Michelle, Nancy Lee, Teenella Simone and Delephia whose time, support, and prayers got me through the next phase of my professional life.

DEDICATIONS

This book is dedicated to my daughter Jasmine who inspires me everyday to continue to live my life in service to others and to deliver my gifts to world that is in need of love and light.

And to every business owner who has a dream of making a greater impact in the world. Nothing is impossible for you if you can believe.

"I literally went from less than $100,000 to over 1.2 million in the first six months of business. Imagine how blown away I was to win my first contract so quickly. It was exciting, it was life-changing and it was awesome.

It can happen to you and it happens fast because there are tools that you can use as a business owner that allow you to do your own searches for the bids that are out there; but you can't play, if you haven't paid as it relates to getting your certification."

Tawanna Heyward-Bey

WELCOME

Welcome to our first
Business Master Class:
Get Certified – Learn The Basics and
Benefits of Becoming a "Certified"
Business Owner.

We congratulate you for taking this first
step into growing your business
through certification.

"There is the risk you cannot afford to take, and there is the risk you cannot afford not to take."

~Peter Drucker

WHY THIS BOOK

For years we have heard the term "knowledge is power". This statement is quite true; however, knowledge without action is nothing! You must be willing to execute what you know or as we use to say at our Weight Watchers meetings......move your body-take some action! Small Business owners and solopreneurs who are looking to get started have been approaching me about certification and business management for years.

As a spiritual person, I do believe that a higher being is always at work for the good of oneself, others and the community. I was thrilled on the afternoon that I received a phone call from LaTania. She had one of my business brochures which listed my minority certifications and she reached out to me for assistance with her own company. That call opened a door of opportunity in itself.

The more we talked and shared with each other, the more apparent it was that we both shared a passion for helping, coaching and training others in business management. With her Wealthy Women Network and my consulting firm, it didn't take us long to move our business experience and talents into action as partners!

We immediately got to work developing and executing audio and training webinars and one day, considering La Tania is already a bestselling author, she hit me with the great idea to co-author the "Get Certified – Learn the Basics and Benefits of Becoming a Certified Business Owner"! Needless to say, the collaboration of putting the basic information in writing about these various certifications has proved to be fulfilling and life changing.

We both have experienced the lack of help, support and just information on how to build and grow your business. We were getting calls and emails from our webinars; it was clear that we needed something more, which is how this book came about.

As entrepreneurs and trainers we know and understand that there are many things to accomplish as business owners and many pit falls waiting for you to fall into.

It is our plan and prayer that you the reader will experience an easy and friendly read; which can help put you on a path of knowledge and success. Let's get started!

Tawanna Heyward-Bey
https://www.heywardbeyinternational.com

INTRODUCTION

Now is the perfect time to explore expanding your small business with the many opportunities that are now available to you through certification. No matter what industry your business may be in the federal government, large companies and/or fortune 500 corporations may an urgent need for your product or service.

Many of these large corporations are not only looking to do business with small business owners like you, but in fact several of them have already made formal commitments to do so.

Therefore if you are a professional, such as an attorney, an accountant or an insurance agent there are large corporations that are in need of your services. If your company sells specialty goods, products or services there is in fact a larger business looking to partner and do business with you. And if you are a small boutique firm and you personally provide services as a graphic artist, a copywriter, public relations or employee training there are opportunities with large companies that are waiting for you.

Large corporations like the Marriott International Inc., and many others have access to a data base of certified women and minority owned small business owners that are qualified to conduct business with them. As a corporate member of the National Minority Supplier Development Council that maintains hotels around the world, the Marriott International Inc. is committed to progressively searching for qualified small businesses with which to partner.

So as you read this book begin to familiarize yourself with the many ways your company can benefit as a certified business owner. Certification can open the door for you to begin working with corporate clients and allow you to expand your business and build your brand.

If no one has ever given you the permission to play a bigger game, if you have never seen yourself doing business outside of your local community, if no one has ever said that you can take your business national or the impact that you have been called to make in the world is needed globally, please allow Tawanna and myself to give you the permission to up your game right now.

We invite you to see yourself as an international player. And the great thing about being in business during this time is that you can play on a larger scale from anywhere in the world and in a way that works best for you.

You can run your business from the comfort of your own home or you can be a person that travels the world making a global impact in your industry. There are tools, strategies and technologies available to you today that will allow you to define success for yourself. There are no barriers or gatekeepers to hinder you from growing your business as fast as you would like. And the only limits that you have are the limitations you place on yourself.

With that being said and your permission being granted Tawanna and I would like to walk you through the basics and many benefits of becoming a certified business owner.

LaTania Michelle

https://www.lataniamichelle.com

 howa

If you don't build your
dream, someone else will
hire you to help them build
theirs.
~*Dhirubhai Ambani*

GOOD NEWS FOR SMALL BUSINESS OWNERS

In the past few years nearly 100 billion dollars has been spent by many of the United States largest corporations to buy goods and services from minority owned small business? Companies like Walmart made over $11 billion in purchases from diverse suppliers and many of these suppliers were women and minority owned small businesses. These companies took the time to expand their business by focusing on

27

meeting the requirements and fulfilling the needs major corporations.

Right now there is a revolution happening in the business-to-business marketplace. There are a profound number of opportunities for women and minority owned small businesses that are ready to expand, grow and compete in the global marketplace.

In a global survey 83% of executives said they are planning to use significantly more outside experts. These large companies have begun to spend billions of dollars with small business owners who have the capacity to service their needs.

This year alone it is estimated that over $36.4 billion will be spent with outside experts for training, coaching and other employee development goods and services.

As these companies have opened their door to small business owners to fill the gap and meet many of their business and supply needs a large number of them have taken steps to make it easier to identify and connect with qualified small business owners by using certification as a third party qualifier.

"The dream is free.....

The hustle is sold separately."

Unknown

THERE IS PLENY OF BUSINESS TO GO AROUND

I've been saying for years that there is enough pie for any small business owner who is willing to work hard to achieve part of that pie. There is no need to be greedy about it either; where you find yourself choking to death and killing or lying on other business owners/your competitors to experience it. Imagine to my surprise as I spent the first year of my business working on my standard operating procedures, business plan, marketing strategies and minority certifications that there are endless opportunities out there and building a multimillion dollar company is possible. As I did my research, I could clearly see that it could be done in the first five years and it didn't have to take decades to achieve it.

Did you know that every federal government purchase anticipated to be valued from $25K to $100K is automatically set-aside for small businesses as long as there are at least two companies that can provide the product or service? These contracts over $100k can be set aside if enough small businesses can provide the service or do the work. Contracts that value over $500k have to include a small business subcontracting plan so that small business or certified minority business can get work under these large contracts.

The government and many public sector entities have an overall goal of 23% of prime contracts flowing to small businesses owners. This is one the greatest benefits to having your certification. *With your certification, you will now have greater access to these opportunities.*

Tawanna Heyward-Bey

ॐ

"Only those who dare to fail greatly can ever achieve greatly."

~Robert F. Kennedy

BIGGER BUSINESS BEGINS NOW

Your journey to becoming a certified business owner starts here and we are excited that you have made the wise decision to learn more about how certification can expand your business.

Government and corporate clients can be vital to the success of your company for many reasons. Your certification can help you obtain these clients and allow you to get your work out into the world in a greater way. Certification will also enable you to strategically obtain more lucrative clients and contracts and can potentially take your business to the next level very quickly.

Again this book is about more than certification.. This book is about expanding your business and preparing you for maximum growth and impact.

So before we go any further let's get clear on the type and scale of business you desire to maintain and the amount of impact you would like to have in your industry. Beginning with the end in mind answer the following questions as we take time to identify and define your business goals.

What is your "Big Vision" for your company?

_____

_____

_____

_____

_____

_____

_____

What is the current revenue for your business? What would you like your revenue to be one year from now?

_____

_____

_____

_____

_____

_____

What would you like your revenue to be in the next 3 years and the next 5 years?

_____

_____

_____

_____

_____

_____

Ideally how many staff members, sub contractors and/or employees would you like to have working within your company? What positions will they hold?

_____

_____

_____

_____

_____

_____

Describe the products and/or services your company provides.

_____

_____

_____

_____

_____

_____

_____

_____

_____

Describe your ideal clients or customers.

_____

_____

_____

_____

_____

_____

Make a list of 5-7 of your ideal clients or companies

_____

_____

_____

_____

_____

_____

_____

How would you like to impact these companies?

_____

_____

_____

_____

_____

_____

What would you like for your company to be known for within your industry.

_____

_____

_____

_____

_____

_____

_____

_____

How much of an impact would you like to make in your industry.

_____

_____

_____

_____

_____

_____

How would you like for your company to benefit your local community, town or state?

_____

_____

_____

_____

_____

_____

_____

_____

_____

_____

_____

Working with corporate and/or government clients will allow you to build a more influential client list. More influential clients can increase your credibility within your industry.

Describe how you believe this influence can affect your business? How would you like to leverage this influence?

_____

_____

_____

_____

_____

_____

_____

_____

_____

How would building your business with certification help you achieve these goals?

_____

_____

_____

_____

_____

"Whatever you can do, or dream you can, begin it. Boldness has genius, power and magic in it."

~*Johann Van Goeth*

WHAT IS CERTIFICATION?

Small business certification is a formal guarantee to corporations that they are purchasing goods and/or services from small business enterprises that meet universal standards for women's (WBEs), minority (MBE), United States veteran, disabled or disadvantaged business enterprises.

Each certification agency conducts a Business Readiness and Certification

Assessment which includes a one-on-one evaluation of the company and whether it meets the universal standards for certification as a small business enterprise. All Small Business Enterprises that successfully complete the process to determine compliance with the certification criteria will earn the Seal of Certification.

Certification does not entitle or guarantee your company will receive any corporate or government contracts. Your small business certification can be used to gain greater access to corporate decision makers and it can open doors to bids and others opportunities from those companies seeking your goods and services

If you are interested in applying for the type of certifications we are outlining in this book, you must first identify the proper certification agency for your business and business goals. Then you must ensure that you meet the eligibility requirements for that agency. At that time you will work that agency to submit an application for review that often includes a site visit and interview.

"The person who really wants to do something finds a way; the other person finds an excuse."

~*Author Unknown*

DOES MY BUSINESS QUALIFY FOR CERTIFICATION?

In this book we will primarily discuss the MBE and WBE programs, but we have also listed a brief outline with the criteria for certification eligibility requirements to obtain additional certifications such as DBE and SBA 8a programs.

The certifications offered by the National Minority Supplier Development Council

(NMSDC), the Women's Business Enterprise National Council (WBENC), and the National Gay & Lesbian Chamber of Commerce (NGLCC) for minority, women, and LGBT-owned businesses, respectively have these general requirements to receive certification.

To determine if your business qualifies for certification ask yourself if your company meets the following four criteria:

_____ Does my business have 51% ownership by one or more women, or minority

_____ Is the day to day and long term control and management of my business by one or more women or minority

_____ Was the primary contribution of capital and/or expertise of my business given by a women or minority individual

_____ Is my business operated independently from other non-certified businesses (ie. Pass-through companies or sales representatives are not eligible.)

CERTIFICATION FOR WOMEN OWNED BUSINESSES

Women Owned Small Businesses may choose to use the services of one of a Third Party Certifiers to certify their business or they may choose to self-certify. The United States Small Business Administration (SBA) has approved four organizations to act as Third Party Certifiers under the Women Owned Small Business (WOSB) Program. The certifying four organizations are:

- El Paso Hispanic Chamber of Commerce
- National Women Business Owners Corporation
- US Women's Chamber of Commerce
- Women's Business Enterprise National Council (WBENC)

The SBA has approved WBENC only for the certification of Women Owned Small Businesses and not for the certification of Economically Disadvantaged Women Owned Small Businesses.

The SBA will only accept third party certification from these entities, and small businesses are still subject to the same eligibility requirements to participate in their programs.

To qualify for certification through the
Women's Business Enterprise National
Council, http://www.wbenc.org/WBE
&WOSB a woman owned small business
must have the following:

- Applicant company must be at least fifty-one
  percent (51%) owned and controlled by one
  or more women who are U.S. citizens or
  lawful permanent residents, or in the case of
  any publicly-owned business, at least fifty-
  one percent (51%) of the equity of which is
  owned and controlled by one or more women
  who are U.S. citizens or lawful permanent
  residents;

- Also, whose management and daily operation
  is controlled by one or more of the women
  owners.

- WBENC uses a two-part process to ensure
  that the applicant company meets the

WBENC Standards. This will include a thorough review of the documentation presented and a site visit interview with the female owner(s).

Note, the United States Small Business Administration (SBA) has approved WBENC as a Third Party Certifier for Women Owned Small Business (WOSB) certification as part of the SBA's WOSB Federal Contracting Program. This certification is for small business owners seeking to become government certified applicants.

The cost for certification and associated fees are determined by each Regional Partner Organization and are based on the specific markets served. Please contact the appropriate RPO directly to determine applicable fees. To do so visit the **Regional**

Partner Organizations territory map on their website and then select your state from the Regional Map to identify the correct RPO for your region/state.

For more information contact the Women's Business Enterprise National Council, http://www.wbenc.org/WBE &WOSB

Bonus Video

www.wealthywoman.org/certification3

Learn the basic requirements for becoming a certified women or minority owned business.
www.wealthywoman.org/certification3

Success isn't something that you do on the outside, success is something that you are on the inside.
The rest will follow.

~Chuck Danes

NATIONAL MINORITY SUPPLIER DEVELOPMENT COUNCIL

The National Minority Supplier Development Council Inc ® (NMSDC®) is one of the country's leading corporate membership organizations. A nonprofit organization The NMSDC® links over 12,000 MBEs with more than 1,750 corporate members, including America's top publicly- owned, privately-owned and foreign-owned corporations, as well as universities, hospitals and other large purchasing organizations.

The organization provides certified MBEs the access, technical assistance, training and support they need to expand and market their services to prospective corporate buyers. The mission of the NMSDC is to advance business opportunities for certified minority business enterprises and to connect them to corporate members. To achieve this mission, the NMSDC:

1. Works through the NMSDC Network to support and facilitate MBE integration into corporate and public-sector supply chains;

2. Builds MBE capacity and capabilities through our programs and other education offerings; and

3. Facilitates MBE-to-MBE partnerships to meet the needs of our corporate members.

The NMSDC has 24 affiliate regional councils nationwide who are committed to the advancement of Asian, Black, Hispanic and Native American suppliers. Their corporate membership includes many of the largest public and privately-owned companies, healthcare companies, colleges and universities in the country.

Here are the requirements for certification with the National Minority Supplier Development Council:

- United States citizens.
- Minority businesses must be at least 51% minority-owned operated and controlled. For the purposes of

NMSDC's program, a minority group member is an individual who is at least 25% Asian, Black, Hispanic or Native American. Minority eligibility is established via a combination of screenings, interviews and site visits. Ownership, in the case of a publicly-owned business, means that at least 51% of the stock is owned by one or more minority group members.

- Must be a profit enterprise and physically located in the U. S. or its trust territories.

- Management and daily operations must be exercised by the minority ownership member(s).

Life is 10% what happens to me and 90% of how I react to it.

~Charles Swindoll

ADDITIONAL CERTIFYING AGENCIES

Here are some of the additional agencies who can help your company become certified as being an Ethnic Minority, Women, Veteran or Service Disabled Veteran Owned Business Enterprise.

United States Department of Transportation, DBE Disadvantage Enterprise Programs

The U.S. Department of Transportation's DBE (disadvantaged business enterprise) program provides a vehicle for increasing the participation by MBEs in state and local procurement. DOT DBE regulations require state and local transportation agencies that receive DOT financial assistance, to establish goals for the participation of DBEs.

Each DOT-assisted State and local transportation agency is required to establish annual DBE goals, and review the scopes of anticipated large prime contracts throughout the year and establish contract-specific DBE subcontracting goals. Also, contracts for businesses that are DBE certified are always available because government entities which receive funding from the Department of Transportation (DOT), are required to make contracts available to companies with a DBE certification. The Federal Aviation Administration (FAA), the Federal Transit Administration (FTA) and the Federal Highway Administration (FHWA) are also required to make contracts available to companies with a DBE certification.

All state and local government entities who are recipients of funds from the FAA and FTA must have a DBE program if they plan to award contracts exceeding $250,000. All recipients of Federal FHWA funds must have a DBE program regardless of projected contract amounts.
http://www.dot.gov/osdbu/disadvantaged-business-enterprise/history-dot-dbe-programo qualify for the United States

Department of Transportation, DBE Disadvantage Enterprise Programs your business must:

- Firm must be at least 51% owned and controlled by a socially and economically disadvantaged individual(s)
- The disadvantaged owners must be an United States Citizen or lawfully admitted permanent resident of the United States
- Firm must be a small business that meets the Small Business Administration's size standard and does not exceed $22.51 million in gross receipts for DBEs
- Personal Net Worth for all owners claiming disadvantaged status for the

DBE and/or ACDBE program must not exceed $1.32 million.

- Firm must be organized as a for-profit business

For more information contact http://www.dot.gov/osdbu/disadvantaged-business-enterprise

Small Business Administration, SBA 8(a) Certification Program

Generally, to be approved into the 8(a) BD program and become certified, your small business must be owned and controlled at least 51% by socially and economically disadvantaged individuals who are American citizens.

- You should also be able to demonstrate potential for business success and possess good character.

*You can visit a small business incubator/learning center or your local small business administration office for assistance with this certification program and any associated fees.

https://www.sba.gov/category/navigation-structure/8a-business-development-program
https://www.sba.gov/blogs/sbas-8a-certification-program-explained

All of the certifications bring value and allow your company access into doing business with corporate, public and government entities. Do your homework. Each certification brings different criteria's, benefits and opportunities as a certified business owner. An additional resource for government opportunities is www.fedbizopps.gov.

A complete list of national, state and regional agencies can be found in DIR's annual Supplier Diversity Information Resource Guide.

- National Women Business Owners Corporation (NWBOC)

- National Minority Supplier Development Council (NMSDC) Regional Councils

- California Public Utilities Commission (CPUC) M/WBE Clearinghouse

- Canadian Aboriginal Minority Supplier Council

- Canadian Gay and Lesbian Chamber of Commerce (CGLCC)

- National Gay and Lesbian Chamber of Commerce

- SBA 8(a) Program

- SBA HUBZone Program

- SBA Women-Owned Small Business (WOSB) & Economically Disadvantaged Women-Owned Small Business (EDWOSB)

- US Pan Asian American Chamber of Commerce

- VETBIZ-Veteran Owned Small Business (VOSB)/Service Disabled Veteran Owned Small Business (SDVOSB)

- WEConnect International

- WEConnect Canada

- Women's Business Enterprise National Council (WBENC)

- US Business Leadership Network (USBLN)

Standardized Self Certification Form - Small, Small Disadvantaged Business (SDB), Veteran Owned Small Business (VOSB), and Serviced Disable Veteran Owned Small Business (SDVOSB)

*Certification fees vary by council and can be found on their individual websites. *Documentation to support claims will also be required.*

Free Bonus Video

www.wealthywoman.org /MBE1

Learn the benefits of becoming a certified WBE (Women Business Enterprise) or MBE (Minority Business Enterprise), Learn how to qualify your business for certification and the types of certification available for your business.
www.wealthywoman.org /MBE1

Every great dream begins with a dreamer. Always remember, you have within you the strength, the patience, and the passion to reach for the stars to change the world.

~Harriet Tubman

BENEFITS TO BECOMING A *"CERTIFIED"* SMALL BUSINESS

Access is the greatest benefit to becoming certified as a business owner. Certification gives WBE, WOSB, MBE, DBE, SBA 8(a) exclusive access to purchasing agents, supplier diversity programs, premium networking events, pre bid meetings, and searchable supplier databases. Certified business owners also have access to affordable or free consulting services, training, technology programs, new business relationships and introductions to nationally known corporations.

Many fortune 500 and 1000 companies in the United States have supplier diversity programs which are designed to encourage the use of minority, women, veteran, LGBT (Lesbian, Gay, Bi-Sexual or Transgender), disable veteran owned, historically underutilized business and small business vendors.

Many of these corporations actually go through great measures to do business with certified companies. Some are even legally obligated to. Supplier Diversity programs are apart of many corporations fundamental business strategy to identify and work with minority owned businesses that have received the seal of certification.

If you possess a MBE or WBE (Minority Business Enterprise, Woman-Owned Business Enterprise) certification these programs are specifically designed for large companies to source products and services from you company. Certification can also significantly help your business gain access to government, public and corporate contracts as well.

Whether you are just starting out as a business owner or your company is already established, you can significantly benefit from the "set aside" contracts many government entities possess and/or the supplier diversity programs held by companies in the private sector.

Here is a list of additional benefits of your certification:

> Get listed in the National Supplier Database

- Distinguish yourself from your competitors
- National and Local Networking Events
- Access to a current list of supplier diversity and procurement executives (Women's Council)
- Advocacy Assistance and Guidance
- Pre-Bid meeting invitations and list of prime/general contractors that attend
- RFP/RFB Leads and email Alerts

- Newsletters
- Participate on Social Media with some of certifying agencies
- Education Programs
- Training Webinars
- Mentor-Protégé pairings and other educational or development programs
- Awards (i.e. Supplier of the Year, Leadership Excellence)
- Business Development Programs
- Capacity Building Development and Initiatives
- Roundtable meetings
- Community Contacts and opportunities
- Winning Contracts

These many benefits can ultimately set you apart from other businesses. I learned early, as a business owner, that the opportunities were out there. I also found that some companies may have a hard time meeting their government and company mandated percentage goals to spend due to a variety of reasons, such as investment, awareness, lack of capacity or exposure to contractor association list.

There are no favors given in this process and even though you don't need to have a college degree to get a certification, you must follow and meet all of the criteria rules.

Certifications specialist do their homework, they perform site visits and check out your paperwork and references. I highly recommend you lead out by bringing your

"A" game; which means you have your company ducks in a row. Clients are assuming robust performance and products from small business that have obtained their certification.

ဆာ၏

"You were designed for accomplishment, engineered for success and endowed with the seeds of greatness."

Zig Ziglar

IS CERTIFICATION RIGHT FOR YOUR BUSINESS?

There are several questions you should consider before initiating the certification process. Here are a few things to consider:

Does your business meet the requirements for ownership and operation? Carefully review the requirements for your certification application to ensure a positive outcome.

Each certification committee considers all evidence presented in an application when making a certification decision, so one "negative" answer does not necessarily make your business ineligible. If you have questions regarding specific criteria contact your certification agency for assistance prior to submitting your application.

Does your company have the capacity to fill large contracts while maintaining quality? Corporations and government agencies expect their suppliers to maintain high standards of quality while meeting project specifications and deadlines, often on a very large scale. Having flexible production and staffing capacity is a common requirement for many corporate opportunities. If your company is small, consider the possibility of building strategic alliances with other businesses that have obtained certification before going after large corporate contracts.

Are you willing to share detailed information about your company, including financial and governance documentation, with a third-party agency? Each certification agency places a high priority on maintaining the confidentiality of your documents. In order to identify your eligibility for certification, each Certification Committee requires detailed information about your business. If you are unwilling to furnish all requested documentation, your business may be denied certification.

Are you prepared to incorporate the certification into a long-term business building strategy? It is important to understand that certification is not a direct entitlement or guarantee to corporate contracts. In order to win new business with your certification, you must research appropriate opportunities within corporations, build relationships with procurement representatives, and be patient.

Remember, there are no favors given in this process and prime or general contractors will not just give you a contract if your business certified. Although there are many opportunities, your company must be prepared to receive and maintain them.

Small business certification can give you access; but the competition can be very high. Your certification may get your business in the door, but diligent research, solid relationship building and strong internal best practices will be required to achieve success.

CERTIFICATION READINESS

Corporate members have identified 10 key factors in evaluating a company's capacity to access their supply chains. Those 10 factors are:

1. Up to date governance documents
2. Tax returns for three years
3. Website and email address
4. Insurance
5. Business Plan/ Marketing Plan
6. Dun & Bradstreet Number
7. Up to date financial statements/ Audited financial statements
8. Payment and Invoicing systems
9. Hiring and firing procedures
10. Loans or financing/Line of credit

"I have not failed. I've just found 10,000 ways that won't work."

~Thomas Edison

I AM CERTIFIED NOW WHAT?

Certification can significantly help your business gain access to public, private and government sector contracts. Once you obtain your certification here are some things you want to immediately get done. Keep in mind that whether you are just starting a business or your company is already established, you can drastically benefit from these "set aside" contracts. For

example, there are several government
agencies at the local, state or federal level
which offer certification. If you are serious
about allowing a certification to expand your
business......get started, and this is how you
begin:

1. Get registered with ember entities
   associated with your certification. This
   will register your company in their
   procurement database and to access
   their procurement process. For
   example, your local city, county, school
   districts, water or utilities companies,
   transportation, airport and hospitals. It
   is a lengthy online vendor process, but
   it is highly recommended. You can
   check periodically that your firm
   information is correct in these
   databases.

2. If you want to do business with private-sector buyers, connecting with your NMSDC (National Minority Supplier Development Council). They have regional councils nationwide and will provide you with their standard application and help you get started with the process. The council has many corporate members like MGM, IBM, Verizon, and the Marriot and they connect to over 17,000 minority-owned suppliers.

3. Get to know the general contractors and prime contractors and others in your industry and within your area and ask them to contact you and notify you of upcoming bids and contracting opportunities.

4. Maximize your certification exposure by participating in your certification entity outreach activities, training sessions and networking events.

5. Obtain notice of bid opportunities. You can become aware of bid and opportunities by online bid postings, local newspapers, online bid search engines and bidder's hotlines. *(Note, learn how to properly respond to these bids; which are called RFP = Response for Proposals or RFB = Response for Bids)* Contact us, we offer consulting/training on this.

6. Attend Pre-Bid meetings, pass out your business card to everyone and network, network, network. This is a great

opportunity to meet prime or general contractors who may want to work with you in a sub-partner relationship.

7. Be pro-active and contact potential prime or general contractors. Your small business may be a great fit as a sub-partner or sub-contractor to a principle or prime contractor.

A prime contractor is the chief business who has a contract with the owner of a project. Prime contractors has the full responsibility for the project's completion. A prime contractor can hire multiple sub-contractors and is responsible for the day-to-day oversight of each sub-contractor of the project. Managing vendors and communicating information to all involved parties throughout the course the project is also the important role of a prime contractor.

8. Visit buyers to assess the needs of the potential corporate clients. Ask lots of questions, they give great advice on how to work with them and respond to their bids.

Don't delay! Your certification is more than a piece of paper you place in a frame and hang on the wall in your office. Do the work and let your certification begin to work for you and your business.

1. List three things you can do today to get started on your certification?

_____

_____

_____

_____

_____

_____

_____

_____

2. What five large corporations would you like to do business with in your city/state?

_____

_____

_____

_____

_____

_____

3. What five entities can you register your company with today?

_____

_____

_____

_____

_____

_____

_____

_____

4. Are you familiar with term RFP, RFQ, RFB or RFI?

_____

_____

_____

_____

_____

_____

_____

5. On a scale of 1-10 how well can you respond to a RFP (Request for Proposal) Bid today?

_____

_____

_____

_____

_____

_____

_____

_____

6. What training would you need to improve your rating in these areas?

_____

_____

_____

_____

_____

_____

7. Is there anything holding you back from getting started today? If so, what steps can you take to get past it?

_____

_____

_____

_____

_____

_____

_____

_____

8. Are you ready to get in the game with your "A" game?

_____

_____

_____

_____

_____

_____

ಬಾಡ಼

"Where success is concerned, people are not measured in inches, or pounds, or college degrees, or family background; they are measured by the size of their thinking."

~ David Schwartz

Is a Home Office Right For You
Tawanna Heyward-Bey

There are many business professionals who make the decision to become their own boss or embark on entrepreneurship working to bootstrap their way to success. This decision is exciting and complex because you must decide where to conduct your business and establish an office; which can be extremely challenging.

To avoid the expensive cost associated with renting an office or leasing office space for at least a minimum of one year many business owners decide to work from home. The Ultimate Home Office can be created for maximum productivity as you build your business.

Here are some key strategies and advice to implement and consider while setting up an ultimate home office; which can lead to ultimate freedom, tax savings, less stress and cash generating opportunities.

Why A Home Office

First you must consider your actual work space. When setting up the ultimate home office in your home, you must have a room, garage or backhouse that can be dedicated as office space. It is a great mistake to make a living or family room into an office. It is too distracting and will not allow you to have the proper desk space where you can leave important files and confidential information out in the open.

Ergonomic Rules

There is a physical demand that comes with work and the science behind adapting and working safely to avoid back problems or disorders like carpel tunnel and tendonitis should be the focus.

Ergonomics shows how constructive or destructive people function in their work environment. For example, many people who sit at a work station all day tend to slouch when sitting at their desk for long periods of times. An ergonomic chair is great if you want to purchase new equipment. The main goal of ergonomics rules is to achieve comfort which helps to maintain good poster and health. Ergonomics is a way of realizing the harm and designing was to prevent it from occurring in the first place. The goal is your safety.

Items or Supplies Needed

There are some specific items or office supplies you need to create the ultimate home office. A good and practical list would be:

- Computer – laptop computers are flexible, but if you have a dedicated workspace, you can save by buying a desktop computer system
- Telephone – if you share your phone with the rest of the family, consider a

two-line cordless phone that has call
display

- Printer (multi-function printers also
  act as a fax and photocopier)
- Fax – consider a multifunction
  printer so that you don't have a fax and
  a printer cluttering your office
- Internet connection – consider
  wireless Internet
- Filing cabinets – keep working files on
  your desktop, but make sure you have
  somewhere to keep business records.
  You need to keep tax records for seven
  year also have the key for confidential
  items
- Book Shelve – for your professional
  library, great place for pictures,
  trophies and awards

- Desk or home office armoire – get an ergonomic one that's set at the right height
- Chair – get a chair that's suited to heavy long-term use
- Stationery, stapler and supplies – envelopes, business cards, printer paper, paperclips and the like
- Calendar – schedule appointments with your computer or PDA, but keep a hardcopy in a calendar or appointment too
- In-box (and an outbox) – stacking trays help you manage incoming and outgoing paper
- Home business permit from your local municipality, if applicable

Netiquette

Communication with others on social, media, cell phones, text messaging without misunderstanding can be challenging. Netiquette rules in technology are crucial for safety and professional reasons.

Rule number two is to adhere to the same standards of behavior on line that you follow in real life. Sometimes people violate these netiquette rules because it is easier to speak their mind without regard to professionalism or building great relationships. It is very difficult to get a clear view of someone tone
(especially if you don't know them personally) and keeping in mind the core rules of netiquette are essential to

maintaining cordial and professional
behavior.

There are ten rules that stand
out greatly. These rules are:

- Rule 1: Remember the Human
- Rule 2: Adhere to the same
  standards of behavior online that
  you follow in real life
- Rule 3: Know where you are in
  cyberspace
- Rule 4: Respect other people's
  time and bandwidth
- Rule 5: Make yourself look good
  online
- Rule 6: Share expert knowledge
- Rule 7: Help keep flame wars
  under control
- Rule 8: Respect other people's
  privacy

- Rule 9: Don't abuse your power
- Rule 10: Be forgiving of other people's mistakes

Hardware, Software and Network Configuration

The most necessary item needed to get work done with the Ultimate Home Office is your Network technologies and the software you will use. There are a variety of options and the most common type of network technology are wireless.

Regardless to the business you will conduct with your home office, it is necessary to have either a desk top computer, lap top or tablet. You may also need to download various software packages to conduct your business.

When working in the Ultimate Home office, the old adage is "time is money" and this rings true when it comes to internet speed. This office cannot afford poor reception for Skype and face to face conference calls.

Therefore, every Ultimate Home Office requires a Network Configuration. Wi-Fi or internet service that will provide fast and efficient internet access. After some research, it's noted that Best Buy has some great and reasonable prices for the computers and Microsoft Office Suite software needed. Microsoft will be used primarily for word, excel and PowerPoint presentations. Finally, Google Chrome is one of the most popular web browsers today. It is fast and has a simple user interface.

Home Office Summary

There are more and more individuals choosing the Ultimate Home office as an option to getting out of the corporate rat race to become their own boss. Many business owners and entrepreneurs are discovering the many benefits like personal financial freedom, increased opportunities, tax advantages, less stress and risk as well as more time for friends and family.

When you follow the basic rules with your work space, ergonomics, adequate supplies, netiquette and reasonable priced equipment and software you can have a great set up which can last you for many productive years.

Launching an Ultimate Home Office can be an opportunity of a life time giving birth to your desire of freedom and your passions and hobbies creating a money-generating outlet for your unique and creative talents. Good luck!!

Certification Resources

Association of Women's Business Centers:
http://abc.biz
Supporting women in geographically
disadvantaged areas and their businesses

Center for Veterans Enterprise:
http://vetbiz.gov
Supporting United States Veterans in
business endeavors, certification, grants, etc.

Center for Women's Business Research:
http://ncrw.org
An organization increasing opportunities for
female business owners across the globe;
publishing reports, stats and insider
information

Diversity information Resources:
http://diversityinforesources.com
Offering directories, reports and resources
full of information about the nation's
registered minority business owners,
associations, diversity groups

Entrepreneur Connect:
http://econnet.entrepreneur.com
Entrepreneur Magazine's program connects
business owners worldwide and facilitates
networking and exchange of trade statistics
and global industry information

The Entrepreneurs' Organization:
http://eonetwork.org
A global entrepreneur membership network

Fortune Magazine Small Business:
http://fortunesb.com

IBM Global Supply Chain Officer Study:
http://www-
935.ibm.com/services/us/bgs/bus/html/gbs
-csco-study.html
IBM's annual report, highlighting data,
analysis, and trends from the top supply
chain officers; important information
pertaining to suppliers, outside services,
vendors, etc

MBE Connect: http://www.mbeconnect.com
Networking and connecting for minority-owned business enterprises

Microsoft Small Business Center: http://microsoft,com/smallbusiness
Resources, statistics, and the latest tools to support your business

National Association for Self-Employed: http://nase.org
Leading micro-business research and membership benefit packages for your business

National Association of women Business Owners: http://nawbo.org
Certification requirements and WBE resources available: national local chapters

National Minority Business Council, Inc: http://www.nmbc.org
Obtain minority certification, local networking and business development information

National Minority Supplier Development council, Inc: http://www.nmsdc.org
Provides direct links between minority business owners and corporations

National Women's Business Council: http://www.nwbc.org
Find membership information, obtain certification, local and national networking

SCORE: http://www.score.org
Local events, networking, and business tools for entrepreneurs – especially veterans minority-owned business, women business owners, and geographically disadvantaged entrepreneurs

Supplier Connection: http://supplier-connection.net
Headed by IBM, Supplier Connection links big and small businesses together to form partnerships and increase opportunities for entrepreneurs to work as suppliers to large lucrative clients

WEConnect International:
http://weconnectinternational.org
A corporate-led non-profit organizations
leading the way on international women-
owned business development and insights

Women's Business Enterprise National
Council: http://www.wbenc.org
Obtain certification, local and national
networking, regional chapter support

Heyward-Bey International "Building Your
Business" Online Business School
www.heywardbeyinternational.com
Learn everything from starting and growing
a thriving business, with a solid foundation
to how to **"GET CERTIFIED"** and learn
how to leverage your certification to winning
6 to 7 figure contracts by bidding on, Fortune
500 Corporations, public municipality or
government contracts! Some course topics
are: "First things First" – Preparing For
Business , From Passion to Non-
Profits, Human Resources, Joint
Ventures, "A-Game" Ready Presentations for
your clients and so much more.
This six months coaching program is
changing lives! Get enrolled today.

Here is additional information for your business library

1. http://web.sba.gov/glossary/
2. http://entrepreneurs.about.com/cs/generalresources/a/glossaryindex.htm

3. http://www.myownbusiness.org/business_glossary.html

4. http://www.entrepreneur.com/article/49490

5. http://www.small-business-dictionary.org/

6. http://www.adversity.net/Terms_Definitions/TERMS/Supplier_Diversity.htm

7. http://www.ethnicmajority.com/Corporate_supplier_diversity_programs.htm

8.
http://www.inc.com/encyclopedia/government-procurement.html

9. http://www.inc.com/encyclopedia/hubzone-empowerment-contracting-program.html

ᔥᐯᖇ

"We cannot hold a torch to light another's path without brightening our own."

~Ben Sweetland

SUCCESS SECRETS TO GROW YOUR BUSINESS

1. Build your business around your gifts, talents, purpose and dreams. Because it may seem like a great way to make money, many people build a business that does not bring them personal joy, fulfillment or happiness. Don't just build a business Design A Life. A life you will love.

2. Identify the reasons why this business is important to you and why you desire

to be successful. Staying focused on these core elements of your goals will help to move you past the obstacles and challenges you will face as a business owner.

It will also give you the discipline needed to stay the course as you take the small steps needed to accomplish your dreams.

3. Make a commitment to grow as a person before you grow your business. You can only advance your company as you develop your personal leadership, communication and people skills.

It takes an extra ordinary person to grow an extraordinary business.

Commit to becoming an extraordinary person.

4. Surround yourself, collaborate and build partnerships with other business owners who have big dreams. But also make sure they have similar passions, desire to serve others and to grow both financially and spiritually.

It is true that you become the average of the five people you spend the most time with. Your associations will make all the difference in your world.

5. Delegate, delegate, delegate. Learn to value YOUR time more than any other asset you possess. Successful business owners develop the habit of outsourcing and delegating all non-

critical activities. Any task that does not require your personal attention can be assigned to someone who may be more gifted or efficient allowing you the opportunity focus on working on your business and in your business.

6. Over deliver. The best way to get your clients to becoming a raving fan is to give more than is expected. Create systems in your business that allows you to exceed your client's expectations.

7. Give back. Giving is a powerful universal principle that allows you to use your business to make a difference in the lives of others and not just your clients. Commit to regularly giving a portion of your profits, time and

talents to a cause that you are passionate and you will be glad you did.

ഇരു

"There are no elevator to success....

You have to take the stairs. "

~ Zig Ziglar

THE MINDSET OF SUCCESS

All success and/or failure begins and ends with your mindset. Reaching your goals in any area of your life starts with you, how you think and what you believe. Therefore putting yourself into the right frame of mind, staying focused and remaining positive are vital components to obtaining and growing your business.

Here are a few business building affirmations that can help you create a mental picture of success as you grow your business with certification.

"I believe in myself and the value that I have to offer my clients and customer".

"I am great at what I do; I deliver great value while making a profit doing so."

"Companies and corporations are looking for my products and services and I easily connect to the right clients at the right time"

"My work is powerful, it helps others and transforms lives."

"I have what it takes to service my clients with excellence."

Recommended Reading for Your Personal and Business Development Library

Tawanna's Recommendations

- The Real Truth about Success by Garrison Wynn
- Think and Grow Rich by Napoleon Hill
- The Trusted Advisor by David H. Maister, Charles Green & Robert Galford
- The Founder's Dilemmas: Anticipating and Avoiding the Pitfalls That Can Sink a Startup by Noam Wasserman
- The 21 Indispensable Qualities of A Leader by John C. Maxwell

LaTania's Recommendations

- The 21 Irrefutable Laws of Leadership by John C. Maxwell
- Fascinate: Discover the best of how the world sees you by Sally Hogshead
- The Millionaire Master Plan by Roger James Hamilton
- The Millionaire Messenger by Brendon Burchard
- Purpose Awakening by Toure' Roberts

Notes

Notes

Notes

Notes

About The Authors

Tawanna Heyward-Bey

Tenacious, dynamic, passionate, fearless, experienced leader are some words you will hear to describe Entrepreneur Tawanna Heyward-Bey. She began her career as an Entrepreneur after spending twenty plus years working in Non-Profit organizations and Corporate America.

She has had notable contracts with companies like Bombardier Transportation, DFW International Airport, Follett Software, Blumberg Excelsior, Molina Healthcare, North Texas Tollway Authority and many others.

With contracts in the public, private and government sectors; Ms. Heyward-Bey strongly believes that building and growing your business into the millions *"can be done"* and is often quoted as she shares this message as a public speaker, advocate and expert trainer for Small Business Enterprise owners across the country on the certification process.

For more information on how you can book Tawanna for public speaking, coaching
you in growing your business, workshops, or training for your organization you can email her at
heywardbeycoach@gmail.com or
book a **FREE 45 minute discovery call**
at https://app.acuityscheduling.com/sched ule.php?owner=16043336

Also, connect with Tawanna Heyward-Bey on the following:
Website:
www.heywardbeyinternational.com
Instagram:
www.instagram.com/theywardbey/
Twitter:
https://twitter.com/theywardbey
Facebook:
https://www.facebook.com/Heyward-BeyInternational/
LinkedIn:
https://www.linkedin.com/in/tawannaheyw ardbey/

LaTania Michelle

LaTania Michelle Smith is a business development and confidence coach. She is an author and speaker. Her experiences as a business woman, mentor, coach, mother and friend has given her an insight into what it takes to overcome great obstacles and turn impossibilities into possibilities.

As the Founder of the Wealthy Woman's Network, LaTania has touched the lives of many across the country and overseas, with a passion, for releasing the unlimited potential that lies within.

LaTania is the recipient of a number of awards for both business and ministry including: the Life Time Achievement Award from Crenshaw Christian Center, and a number of honors from the City of Los

Angeles, the California State Assembly and the California State Senate.

Specializing in leadership, mindset and communication LaTania conducts corporate workshops, keynote address and virtual training in the following topics.

• Leadership Development Training
• Mindset Strategies for an Innovative Workplace
• Management Development
• Communication Skills For Work Place Success
• Confidence Coaching For New Managers
• Team Building and Training

For more information on how you can book LaTania for your business, organization or ministry e-mail her at latania@lataniamichelle.com, visit www.lataniamichelle.com.

Connect with us on www.facebook.com/lataniamichelle

Get Certified – Events

Are you looking to accelerate your success? Attend one of our Get Certified Live or Virtual Events and work with Tawanna and LaTania for an afternoon or entire weekend!

The Get Certified team will take you through the Certification Process one step at a time and put you on the fast track to success!

In these one-on-one or small group events you will identify the appropriate certification for your business and get you started on your certification application. We will also review your required documentation to ensure that you have everything you need for application submission.

You will also leave with a personalized step by step strategy to create strategic alliances and corporate partnerships.

For more information on the Get Certified Live Event contact us online at www.heywardbeyinternational.com.

Corporate and Organizational Training Programs

Would you like to fast-track the success of your company, association or organization?

Our Corporate and Organizational Training Programs are specifically designed to enable you to achieve your goals in record time.

We will help you shatter your organizational speed limits with fast-paced, entertaining and informative seminars and workshops providing you and your team with proven strategies to:

- Increase Innovation and Creativity
- Increase Employee Engagement and Productivity
- Effective Communication
- Dramatically Enhance Teamwork
- Improve Leadership Skills among Your Executive and Management Teams

Visit our website at **www.heywardbeyinternational.com** to learn more about how we can help you and your team make the most of your company's assets.

Possibility Publishing

Possibility Publishing provides our clients with proven systems, resources, and support to produce quality inspirational and professional non-fiction books.

We know getting your own book written, printed and published is a huge project.

We can provide you with an experienced team to put your book into the marketplace. Our authors quickly and affordably reach their audience with the latest strategies and technology available in the publishing industry today.

For information about additional Possibility Publishing books, music, videos, or productions or to get your book published contact us today.

Also visit us online at http://possibilitypublishing.org or give us a call at (310)387-4566

Final Thoughts

We would like to thank you for joining us in our first business masterclass: Get Certified: Learn The Basics and Benefits of Becoming a *"Certified"* Business Owner.

We are here to **coach, consult and cheer** you on to great success in growing your business. Don't delay, get started today.

Tawanna and LaTania

Made in the USA
Columbia, SC
13 January 2023